RAIN MAKES

To Susan, Scott, and Grey
and in memory of Leslie

APPLESAUCE

by

JULIAN SCHEER & MARVIN BILECK

Published 1964 by
Holiday House, New York

The stars are made

of lemon juice

and rain makes applesauce

oh you're just talking silly talk

inside out and rain makes applesauce

My house goes walking

Dolls go dancing

on the moon

and

rain makes applesauce

The wind blows backwards all night

long and

and

rain makes applesauce

Oh you're just talking silly talk

Monkeys mumble

in a jelly bean jungle

and

rain makes applesauce

Candy tastes like

soap soap soap and

rain makes applesauce

OH YOU'RE JUST TALKING SILLY TALK

Monkeys eat

the chimney smoke and

Clouds hide in

Salmon slide

down a Hippo's hide

oh you're just talking sillytalk

and rain makes applesauce

My Teddy Bear sings out

loud at night and rain makes applesauce

on a tickle tree

and

rain

makes applesauce

Oh, you're just talking silly, silly, silly talk.

know I'm talking silly talk... But—

apple-sauce